Contents

Introduction

You can enjoy learning about nature by trying all the exciting and interesting projects in this book. They will give you and your friends days of fun. The projects are easy to understand and simple to do. You will be able to complete many of them by yourself or with a friend. Ask an adult to help if you are unable to do something.

Studying nature is a fascinating hobby that you will never grow tired of. You will learn to love watching plants as they grow, burst into beautiful flowers and then release their seeds so that lots of new plants can grow. It is just as much fun to spy on animals going about their daily lives. You will find out how they move, what they eat and where they like to live.

Looking and learning

People who are interested in nature are called naturalists. Naturalists are born collectors. They gather and study all the wonderful things that nature leaves behind. In autumn, leaves of many different shapes and shades fall from the trees. Along the seashore you can find oddly shaped pieces of driftwood, shells and seaweed that have been washed up with the tide. Feathers, fossils and old bones are just a few of the other things that you could look out for. Naturalists use the word specimens for the bits and pieces that they collect.

When you have collected some specimens, you might want to identify exactly what they are and learn more about them. You can buy special books, called field guides, that have pictures and information about animals and plants. If you get really interested in the natural world, a field guide would be very useful.

Naturalists like to identify the specimens they collect with a good field guide. They can then start to put together a proper collection.

A magnifying glass is a very important tool for anyone who is interested in nature. Without one, you will miss many interesting details. Tiny creatures look like fantastic monsters when they are magnified!

Getting close

As you collect more specimens, you will get better at noticing and recognising all kinds of things about them. You may find that you are able to sort your specimens into groups. Try grouping them according to what they look like or where you found them. You can see a lot with your eyes, but even more if you have a magnifying glass. A magnifying glass is a piece of specially shaped glass that makes it easy to see even the tiniest details on a small creature. A whole new world will open up and you will be able to see things that you have never seen before!

Where can you find nature?

The natural world can be found everywhere, even in the most unexpected places, like on the soles of your boots! You just have to keep your eyes open and look carefully at everything around you.

You can find all kinds of things to study right inside your own home. You do not even have to step outside. Tiny creatures and insects can be discovered hiding in the corners of rooms, cut flowers are displayed in vases, houseplants bloom in their pots and pets go about the fascinating business of their daily lives.

SHOW ME HOW
Nature Projects

Fun-to-do projects for kids
shown step by step

STEVE & JANE PARKER

ARMADILLO

This edition is published by Armadillo, an imprint of Anness Publishing Ltd, 108 Great Russell Street, London WC1B 3NA; info@anness.com

www.annesspublishing.com

If you like the images in this book and would like to investigate using them for publishing, promotions or advertising, please visit our website www.practicalpictures.com for more information.

A CIP catalogue record for this book is available from the British Library.

Publisher: Joanna Lorenz
Editors: Lyn Coutts, Ann Kay, Richard McGinlay
Photographer: John Freeman
Stylist: Thomasina Smith
Designer: Rachael Stone
Production Controller: Rosie Anness

We would like to thank the following children, their parents, for appearing in this book: Hazel Askew, Jessica Bawden, Shaunagh Brown, Jamie Grant, Liam Green, Jack Harvey-Holt, Naeve Mulcahy, Georgina Nipah, Abayomi Ojo, Tiffani Ogilvie, Jinsamu Shimizu and Sophie Louise Viner.

PUBLISHER'S NOTE
The amount of help needed from adults will depend on the abilities and ages of the children following the projects. However, we advise that adult supervision is vital when the project calls for the use of sharp knives or other utensils. Always keep potentially harmful tools and substances well out of the reach of young children.
   Although the advice and information in this book are believed to be accurate and true at the time of going to press, neither the authors nor the publisher can accept any legal responsibility or liability for any errors or omissions that may have been made nor for any inaccuracies nor for any loss, harm or injury that comes about from following instructions or advice in this book.

Manufacturer: Anness Publishing Ltd, 108 Great Russell Street, London WC1B 3NA, England
For Product Tracking go to: www.annesspublishing.com/tracking
Batch: 1386-22722-1127

Having fun with this book

The projects in this book will introduce you to nature study in a fascinating way. Most of the specimens and materials that you will need are easy to find. You will have many of them at home already. When you have done some of the projects in this book, you will probably think of other nature study projects to do.

Displaying your finds

Once you have collected your specimens you will want to display them. The Mini Museum is a very easy-to-make display box which will keep small specimens safe and clean. Or you could make a book in which to store your dried or pressed flowers and your leaf and bark rubbings. There are many ways of using your specimens to make gifts and decorations. You can also make all kinds of things just for fun, too, like a Fancy Buttonhole and pictures made of leaves.

Some of your projects will have to be set up outside. The Dustbin Lid Pond, Luxury Bird Treat, Wild Flower Window Box and Butterfly Garden projects are great ways of attracting wildlife to your garden. They will help you to learn more about nature. They are also helping nature by giving creatures food, water and somewhere to live.

Naturalists like to keep records of what they find. Keep a nature notebook and draw pictures of each specimen. Write down where you found it and when, what it looks like, how big it is and how many legs or petals it has.

Out and about

In your garden or local park you can watch all kinds of growing things change dramatically from one season to the next. You might like to keep a nature notebook or a diary of the changing scene in your garden or local park. You could draw what you see or collect and glue your specimens into your notebook. It is important that you write what each specimen is and where and when you found it.

There is even lots to learn when you go to a supermarket. The shelves are full of the things that nature produces, like fruits and vegetables, nuts and seeds, eggs and milk. Trips to the countryside, the seaside, or to a museum or zoo, provide many opportunities for you to collect unusual specimens or to study rare and fascinating creatures.

When you have identified your specimens, you will want to show them off. Make an attractive display of your best specimens. Try to get your friends interested in nature too.

Being nature's friend

Naturalists never want to harm or destroy any living things. They like watching them in their natural environment, or surroundings, without disturbing them. This is what you should do too. If you do not, there will be fewer and fewer natural things for you and other people to enjoy.

Caring for animals

Here are some rules about looking after animals –
• Never harm or kill animals.
• Handle small animals with great care. They are delicate and easily squashed.
• Keep animals in safe containers. These containers must have enough holes in them to let in air, so that your animals can breathe.
• If you are going to keep animals for a little while, you must always make sure that they have enough water and suitable food.
• Keep any animals you are watching in a cool place and never let them get too hot.
• Only keep animals for a few hours or days. Then you must return them to where you found them.
• Only catch small animals like insects, worms and snails.
• Do not try to capture larger animals like birds or snakes. Instead, study them from a distance. You could watch them with binoculars or even take photographs. The most important thing to remember is not to frighten or disturb the animal.

If you are keeping animal specimens for a little while, give them a good home. They should be in a safe container, with holes to let in air and plenty of food and water.

Here is a beautiful bouquet of wild flowers using nothing more than common weeds and garden flowers. Always ask permission before you pick flowers from a garden.

Caring for plants

How to care for plants –
• Do not dig up plants by the roots.
• Do not pick or disturb flowers in the wild in any way. There are special laws protecting many wild flowers.
• For flower projects, use common weeds like buttercups and dandelions, flowers from a garden or from a supplier.
• Always ask permission from an adult before you pick any flowers from a garden.
• Put flowers in water until you are ready to use them.

Caring for the environment

Once you have discovered the wonders of the natural world you can learn to care for it properly. You will realize how easily plants, animals and wild places can be destroyed. You will know about looking after animals and plants. Knowing how to live in harmony with nature is very important.

Do not waste anything natural. Even food scraps can be made into compost that will help plants to grow! Does your family do what it can for the natural world? Ask if you can help to take cans, bottles, paper and plastic to local recycling sites so that they can be used again.

Looking after yourself

As well as looking after the natural world, look after yourself when you are out and about enjoying nature –
• When you are handling plants and compost, it is a good idea to wear rubber gloves or gardening gloves. These will keep your hands clean and protect them against any stings or infection.
• A few small animals might sting or scratch, which is why you should handle them with care and wear gloves!
• Some plants are poisonous or can irritate and sting the skin. Ask an adult which ones are safe for you to pick.
• Never eat any part of a wild plant, especially the berries and seeds – they can be poisonous.
• Do not go off on country walks on your own. You should always be with an adult or a much older friend. Besides, you do not need to go far to find specimens – there are plenty in your own back yard!

Never go out for a walk on your own. Ask an adult or much older friend to go with you. If you need to go to the local park or to another person's garden to collect specimens, you must always tell an adult where you are going and when you will be back. Do not stay out for long and always use marked paths. Do not be tempted to go exploring. You might get lost.

The Country Code

When you are out in the country, remember the Country Code –
• Never go alone and always tell an adult where you and your friends are going.
• Never disturb any wild plants or animals.
• Keep to the paths.
• Take care on narrow roads where there is no footpath.
• Keep away from farm animals.
• Leave gates as you found them.
• Never leave refuse behind or start fires.
• Do not go near water alone.
• Keep dogs under control.

All the projects in this book are perfectly safe to do. Always wear gardening or rubber gloves when handling soil mixes, looking for specimens or working in the garden. They will keep your hands clean and protect them from scratches or stings.

Materials

You will need various pieces of equipment to make the projects on the following pages. Some of these items can be used again when you invent your own nature study activities. So that you have your equipment always at hand, why not store them in a special box?

Absorbent kitchen paper This is thick paper that will soak up water and other liquids. Use it when drying pressed flowers and to clean your work table.

Electrical tape This is a very strong sticky tape that is available in lots of different shades. You can buy it from DIY and hardware stores. It is also called insulation tape.

Muslin or cheesecloth This is a very fine cloth that allows air to pass through it very easily. It is used for covering containers that are used to house small creatures.

Non-hardening clay This inexpensive material is available in many shades. It does not harden, so it can be reused.

No-peat compost This is a special soil mixture in which seeds are planted. Often referred to as peat-free multi-purpose compost, it is available from garden suppliers or DIY stores.

Plastic bag Clear plastic bags can be used for carrying specimens and for covering seeds when they are germinating, or growing. Whenever possible, reuse the plastic bags that you are given in supermarkets. Never use plastic bags to cover the top of an animal home.

Plaster-of-Paris powder This is a fine white powder that sets hard when water is added. Use it to make casts of specimens. You can buy it in hobby and toy suppliers.

Plastic drinks bottle By using empty plastic drinks bottles in your projects, you are helping nature by recycling. Ask an adult to help you cut plastic bottles in half.

Wild birdseed This is a mixture of seeds and grains that is specially made for wild birds. You can buy it in pet stores and in some nurseries.

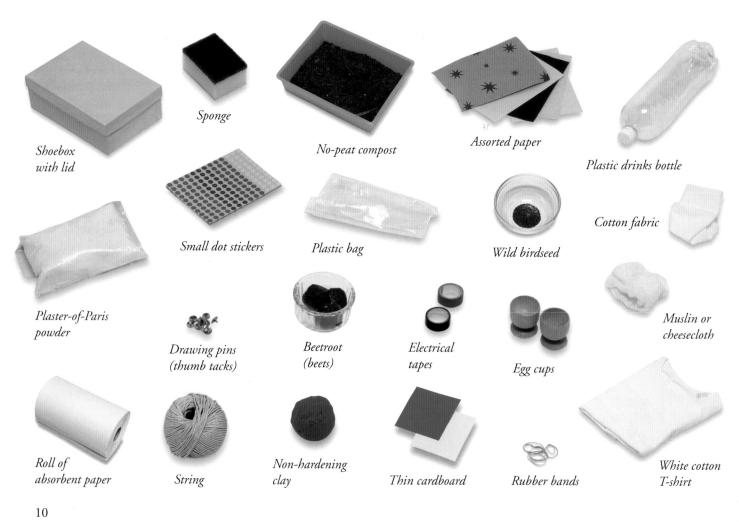

Shoebox with lid

Sponge

No-peat compost

Assorted paper

Plastic drinks bottle

Small dot stickers

Plastic bag

Wild birdseed

Cotton fabric

Plaster-of-Paris powder

Drawing pins (thumb tacks)

Beetroot (beets)

Electrical tapes

Egg cups

Muslin or cheesecloth

Roll of absorbent paper

String

Non-hardening clay

Thin cardboard

Rubber bands

White cotton T-shirt

Watering cans

Water pot

Jam jars

Seed tray

Metal gardening trowel

Plant pot

Plant pot tray

Magnifying glass

Stapler

Rubber boots

Plastic fork

Paints

Paintbrushes

Scissors

Crayons in various shades

White glue

Paper glue

Gardening gloves

Plastic spade

Ruler

Pencils in various shades

Absorbent cloth

Equipment

Jam jars Recycle clean glass bottles by using them as homes for animals. They can also be used as water containers when you are painting.

Gardening gloves These are thick cotton or canvas gloves that are used when gardening. They keep your hands clean and will protect them from stinging plants and insects. Always wear gardening gloves when working with compost.

Magnifying glass This is a specially shaped piece of glass that allows you to see small details on plants and animals. It is an important piece of equipment for a naturalist. A magnifying glass can be bought in hobby and stationery stores.

Metal gardening trowel This can be bought from a garden supplier. Be careful when using a metal tool because the edges are sharp. Ask for permission from an adult before you use any gardening equipment. For some of the projects in this book you can use a plastic beach spade.

Paper glue This glue is specially made for sticking paper together. It can be bought in tubes or in plastic bottles.

Plant pot You will need a plant pot when you are growing seeds. Plants pots can be made of plastic or terracotta. Terracotta is a red clay that has been baked hard.

Plant pot tray This is a shallow dish that fits under a plant pot. It stops water and compost from leaking out.

Rubber boots These boots will stop your feet from getting wet. They will also protect your legs from stinging plants. Wear boots whenever you are out exploring nature.

Seed tray This is a shallow container that is used to grow seeds in. When the seedlings have grown, they are planted into the garden or into a large pot.

White glue Also known as PVA glue, this can be used on paper, wood, plastic or fabric. It is stronger than paper glue.

11

Leafy Gift Wrap

Use leaves that have fallen from trees to make attractive paper for wrapping gifts. Find leaves in as many interesting shapes and sizes as you can. In this project, you will stencil and print. To stencil, you paint around the leaf. To print, you paint the leaf and then press it on to paper.

Veiny leaves

vein

If you rub your finger over the back of a leaf you will be able to feel the veins. When you paint over the veins and press them on to paper they make a lacy pattern. The veins contain a liquid called sap, which carries food around the plant.

In the autumn, the leaves of many plants turn brown, die and fall to the ground. The veins are the thickest parts of a leaf so they rot quite slowly. Look out for a partly rotted leaf that still has its delicate skeleton of veins.

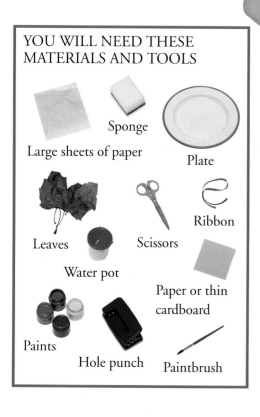

YOU WILL NEED THESE MATERIALS AND TOOLS

Sponge

Large sheets of paper

Plate

Leaves

Scissors

Ribbon

Water pot

Paper or thin cardboard

Paints

Hole punch

Paintbrush

Hazel has wrapped a gift for her friend using handmade wrapping paper. She has also made a beautiful matching gift label.

1 To make a stencil pattern, spread leaves over a large sheet of paper. Mix paint and water on a plate. Use a sponge to dab paint all over the paper.

2 Take the leaves off the paper. Do this carefully, so you do not smudge the paint. The outline of the leaves will be left on the paper.

3 To make a leaf print, paint the back of a leaf with a different shade. Make sure the veins are thickly coated with paint.

4 Place the leaf, paint-side down, into a matching outline on the paper. Use your fingers to press all of the leaf on to the paper.

5 Carefully remove the leaf. You now have your first print. Printing can be messy, so take care not to drip paint over your pattern.

6 Do the same with the other leaves until all the outlines have been filled in. Use different paints for each leaf. Allow the paper to dry.

7 Stencil and print a label. When dry, thread the ribbon though a hole made with a hole punch, or staple the ribbon to the label.

A gift wrapped in handmade paper really is something special! You can decorate all sorts of things using your leafy paper. Use it to cover your school books or your nature notebook.

Mini Museum

All big museums began as small collections. If you start collecting specimens you will soon need somewhere to store them. This shoebox museum will protect specimens from damage and dust. It is also fun and easy to make.

Special specimens

Only collect things that living plants and animals have finished with. These include feathers, leaves, empty seashells, pebbles, open seed heads and hazel nuts. If you are very lucky, you might find a fossil. Always wash your hands after you have been specimen-collecting.

A naturalist would never kill an animal or damage a plant. Never take unhatched birds' eggs or disturb birds' nests. It is cruel and against the law. Take care when collecting – some plants are poisonous and others sting.

Jinsamu shows off his Mini Museum. It is the perfect way to keep his specimens safe and clean.

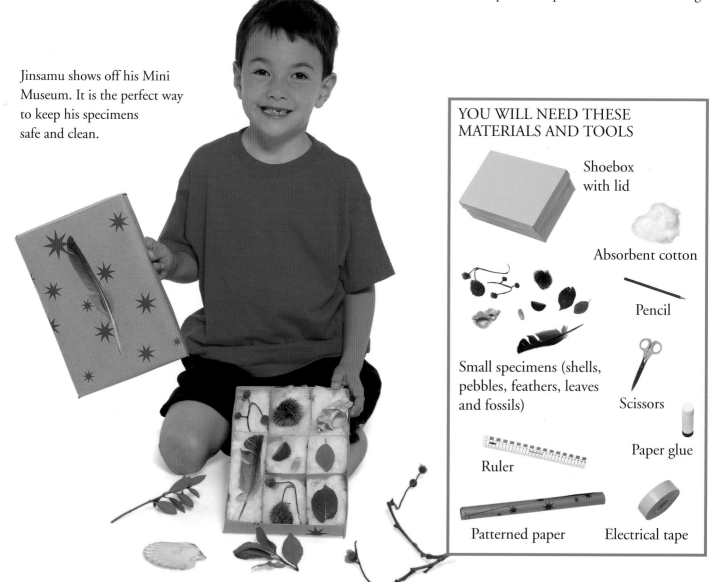

YOU WILL NEED THESE MATERIALS AND TOOLS

Shoebox with lid

Absorbent cotton

Pencil

Small specimens (shells, pebbles, feathers, leaves and fossils)

Scissors

Paper glue

Ruler

Patterned paper

Electrical tape

1 Put the lid on to the bottom of the shoebox. Use a pencil to draw a line carefully around the box, just above the edge of the lid.

2 Remove the lid and cut along the line. Do not cut into the sides of the shoebox. You will need them to make the compartments.

3 Put the shallow box aside. Place the rest of the shoebox in the lid. Draw around it as you did before. Cut along the line and up each corner.

4 You should have four strips of card, each the same depth as the lid. Two pieces are the same length as the box and two are as long as the ends.

5 Divide the strips into three equal sections. Draw lines to mark the sections. Cut half-way across these lines to make slits.

6 Place the slits in the long strips into the slits in the two short strips to make a grid shape, like a game of noughts and crosses or tic-tac-toe.

7 Cover the box and lid with patterned paper. Do not forget to allow enough paper to cover the sides. Stick a leftover specimen on the lid.

8 Fix the grid shape into the shallow box with electrical tape. You may have to trim the ends of each strip to make them fit in easily.

9 Use absorbent cotton to line the compartments. Choose a specimen to go into each compartment. Make labels for your specimens.

Dustbin Lid Pond

Even the smallest pond is wonderful for studying nature. Birds will visit for a drink. Other animals might make it their home and lay their eggs in the water. Then you will be able to watch the young grow.

Be careful!

Ask an adult where to site the pond. You might also need some help to dig the hole. Although this pond is small and shallow, it can still be dangerous. It may carry a rare infection. If you put your hands in the pond, wash them. Do not drink the water.

Sophie welcomes her pond's first visitor, a frog. The pond will look more natural when the water plants are larger and the grass has grown up around the edges.

YOU WILL NEED THESE MATERIALS AND TOOLS

Trowel

Metal or plastic dustbin lid or other shallow container

Rubber boots

Large stones

Pond weed

Water plants

Watering can

Gardening gloves

1 Place the dustbin lid on the ground. Use a trowel to mark a line around the lid. This will make it easy to dig the hole the right size.

2 Move the lid aside. Dig out the soil inside the circular line to about the depth of the lid. Loosen the soil in the hole and put the lid in place.

3 Move the lid backwards and forwards into the hole to settle it down. You must make sure that it is absolutely level.

4 Arrange the stones in the bottom of the dustbin lid. Pile some on top of each other to create an island. Add water plants and pond weed.

5 Use the watering can to fill the pond with tap water. When you do this, try not to disturb your arrangement of stones and plants.

6 Keep the pond full of water. Visit your pond daily to see if any animals have made it their home. They may be very small, so look closely.

7 When your pond has been set up a while, larger animals may arrive. During dry summers, frogs often make garden ponds their home.

Your Dustbin Lid Pond is only small, so do not fill it with too many stones or plants. It is important to keep topping up the water or the animals and plants will die.

Fancy Buttonhole

When people pin one or two flowers on to their clothes like a brooch, it is called a buttonhole. They wear them on special occasions. A buttonhole is best made with several small flowers, or one large flower. This buttonhole has been made using dried flowers that will last for a long time.

Preserving nature
Drying natural things like flowers helps to stop them rotting. When you dry a flower it loses its moisture and will not rot. Use very fresh, young flowers and keep them in water until you are ready to use them. This will stop them wilting.

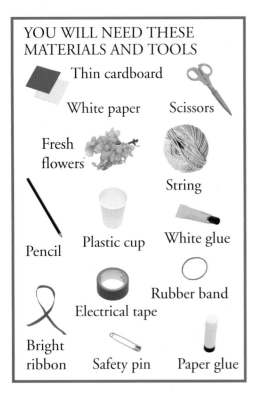

Jack has pinned his buttonhole to his T-shirt. This buttonhole is perfect for wearing to parties or giving as a gift. Large flowers take longer to dry than small ones, so allow extra time.

YOU WILL NEED THESE MATERIALS AND TOOLS

Thin cardboard

White paper

Scissors

Fresh flowers

String

Pencil

Plastic cup

White glue

Rubber band

Electrical tape

Bright ribbon

Safety pin

Paper glue

1 Cut the flower stems very short with a pair of scissors. Arrange the flowers into a tiny bouquet, or bunch. Tie the bunch together with string.

2 Hang the bouquet upside down in a warm and dry place, such as an airing cupboard or linen closet. It will take several days for the flowers to dry.

3 Remove the string from your flowers. Put a rubber band in its place. Twist the band several times to make it tight.

4 Tie the bright ribbon in a bow over the rubber band. Trim the ribbon ends to the right length. Your bouquet is finished.

5 Draw around the cup to make a circle on the card and on the paper. Cut out the circles. Use paper glue to stick the circles together.

6 Attach the safety pin firmly on to the back of the card circle with electrical tape. Make sure that you can open the pin easily.

7 Put a large blob of white glue on to the front of the brooch. Press the bouquet on to the glue. Let it dry before wearing your buttonhole.

Dried flowers have lots of uses. A large bouquet makes an ideal present. You can make flower arrangements in pots and baskets by standing the stems in non-hardening clay. Create a picture by gluing dried flowers on to thin cardboard. Flower petals can be dried using the same method as for drying whole flowers.

Luxury Bird Treat

Encourage birds into your garden with this special bird feeder. Bird-watching is a fascinating hobby that will give you hours of pleasure. Watch them feed and then listen to their bird song.

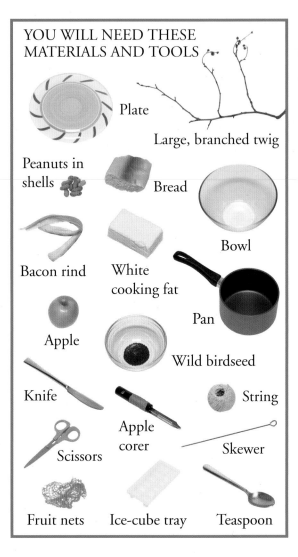

YOU WILL NEED THESE MATERIALS AND TOOLS

Plate

Large, branched twig

Peanuts in shells

Bread

Bowl

Bacon rind

White cooking fat

Pan

Apple

Wild birdseed

Knife

String

Scissors

Apple corer

Skewer

Fruit nets

Ice-cube tray

Teaspoon

Shaunagh is standing under her Luxury Bird Treat. Birds will feed from it when it is hanging in a safe place in the garden.

Bird-watching

You need to be patient to watch birds. You must keep still, quiet and out of sight. When you have been observing birds for some time you get to know their songs and the way they fly. Like us, they also have their fave foods!

The best time to put food out for the birds is in winter. When it is frosty or snowing it is very hard for birds to find enough food. Do not forget that they also need to drink, so provide a shallow dish with some clean water in it.

1 Tie a long length of string to the main stem of your twig. Choose a part of the stem that will make it easy to hang the feeder from a branch.

2 Ask an adult to melt the cooking fat in a pan and pour it into the bowl. Let it cool. Crumble in the bread, then stir in the birdseed.

3 Use the teaspoon to put the fatty mixture into the spaces in the ice-cube tray. Fill each cube to just below the top.

4 Cut lengths of string. Tie a knot in one end of each piece and put the knotted end into each cube. Put the ice-cube tray into the refrigerator.

5 While the cubes are setting, put some of the peanuts into fruit nets (the kind that supermarket oranges are sold in) and cut some string ties.

6 Thread the string in and out of the loops at the top of the net. Pull the string tight and tie it so that it closes like a little purse.

7 Ask an adult to make a hole in some peanuts with a skewer. Thread the nuts on to lengths of string. Tie string around pieces of bacon rind.

8 Core the apple with the corer and slice it very carefully into large rings. Tie a piece of string on to each apple ring.

9 Remove the cubes from the tray and tie all the treats to the twig. Ask an adult to tie it up outside in a place where you can see it.

21

Autumn Leaf Collage

In the autumn it is fun to walk through the fallen leaves and kick them into the air. It is fun to collect them, too. Autumn leaves come in many shades – green, yellow, orange, red and chestnut brown. You can make lovely presents when you use these leaves to create pictures. When you make a picture using bits and pieces, it is called a collage.

Why do leaves go brown?

In the warm summer sun, leaves use up a lot of water as they grow and make food. In the winter, leaves cannot grow and make food because there is little sun and it is cold. Therefore, many trees get rid of their leaves to stop them from wasting water. Before the leaves fall to the ground, the tree absorbs, or takes in, all of their green goodness. This is why autumn leaves go brown.

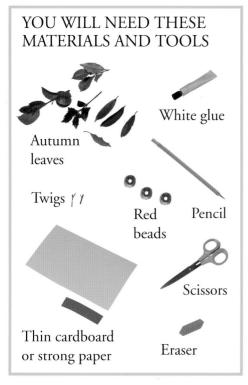

YOU WILL NEED THESE MATERIALS AND TOOLS

Autumn leaves

White glue

Twigs

Red beads

Pencil

Scissors

Thin cardboard or strong paper

Eraser

Hazel's splendid picture is of a magic bird displaying his attractive tail feathers. Hazel is going to give it to her friend for his birthday.

1 Fold your cardboard or paper in half. If you are making a greetings card, write a personal message or glue a picture inside your card.

2 Look at all the different shades and shapes of your leaves. Arrange them carefully to make a picture of a bird on the front of the card.

3 When you have created a picture that you like, draw around it in pencil. This is so that you know where to glue the leaves and twigs.

4 Take the leaves off the card. Then glue them back on, one by one, inside the pencil lines. Press the leaves firmly on to the paper.

5 When you have finished gluing the leaves in position, use an eraser to rub out the pencil lines. Take care not to damage the leaves as you do this.

6 To finish the bird, glue on beads and twigs for the eyes and legs. Cut out a beak and some grass from card. Glue these on to your picture.

7 Allow the collage to dry completely. Trim the picture to the right size. If you want your picture to hang up, tape a loop of string to the back.

You can design all sorts of leaf collage pictures. You could make other kinds of animal pictures, or simply design interesting and bright patterns. Add feathers, pressed flowers, shells, straw and even dried seaweed to your collection of collage materials.

Boot Garden

A lump of soil can contain hundreds of seeds. These may last for many years, just waiting for the weather to be wet and warm enough for them to spring into life. After a walk in your garden, a park or in the countryside, the mud on your boots could be full of seeds. When the seeds are put into damp soil and are left somewhere warm, they will start to grow.

Country walks

Walks in parks and the countryside are lots of fun, but you should always take care. Never go wandering off on your own. It is important that you always go with an adult or a much older friend.

YOU WILL NEED THESE MATERIALS AND TOOLS

Gardening gloves

Muddy boots

Watering can

No-peat compost (soil mix) and plant pot tray

Trowel

Knife

Plastic bag

The seeds in Georgina's Boot Garden have grown and flowered. The mud on her boots came from her auntie's garden that is full of interesting plants and flowers. However, you might be just as lucky if you walk on ground where very little seems to be growing. Who knows what seeds have just blown there?

1 Put some compost into the plant pot tray and pat it down. Leave enough space so that you can add the mud from your boots.

2 Water the compost in your tray thoroughly using the watering can. Seeds need plenty of water to get them to germinate, or grow.

3 Scrape some of the mud from the bottom of your boots on to the top of the compost. It is important that you wear gloves when doing this.

4 Pat the layer of mud down with your trowel. Water the mud if it is very dry. Then carefully slide the tray inside the plastic bag.

5 Twist the end of the bag under the tray to seal it. This will stop the compost and mud from drying out. Put the tray in a warm place.

6 When the seedlings begin to grow, remove the tray from the plastic bag. Leave your Boot Garden in a sunny spot and keep it well watered.

You would never guess that mud could produce flowers! But this project shows that seeds are everywhere. If your first Boot Garden does not produce any plants, try again. You are bound to be successful sooner or later. Soil can carry infections, so wear gloves when you are handling it. Always wash your hands afterwards.

A Book of Flowers

To keep flowers looking beautiful for a long time, you can either dry them or press them. In this project you are going to preserve flowers by pressing them flat and then sticking them in a book. Pressed flowers will keep their appearance for many years if you cover them with sticky-back plastic.

Picking flowers

For this project you can pick flowers from a garden or buy some from a florist. Even weeds can be used for pressing. Ask permission before you take flowers from the garden, and never pick wild flowers. Large flowers contain a lot of liquid. They are messy when pressed and will take much longer to dry.

Jinsamu has a beautiful bunch of flowers in his jam jar, but they will not last as long as the pressed flowers in his book.

YOU WILL NEED THESE
MATERIALS AND TOOLS

Paper glue

Absorbent kitchen paper

Flowers

Paper
or thin
cardboard

Several large books

Thick cardboard

Pencils in
various shades

Scissors

Transparent
sticky-back plastic
(contact paper)

Ribbon

Hole punch

1 Keep the flowers in water until you are ready to use them. Arrange the flowers on several sheets of absorbent paper. Trim any long stems.

2 Check that the flowers are lying flat and that the petals are smooth. Then cover them with several sheets of absorbent paper.

3 Put the flower-and-paper sandwich between two pieces of thick cardboard. Put this on a hard, flat surface and pile the books on top.

4 Leave the flowers under the books for a few days. Then unpack them carefully. They should be flat and completely dry.

5 Glue each flower on to a separate sheet of paper or thin cardboard. Write the flower's name, where you found it and the date on the sheet.

6 Cut two pieces of cardboard the same size as the sheets of paper to make covers. Punch holes in the covers and sheets. Tie together with ribbon.

7 Decorate the cover with drawings of flowers and perhaps a spare pressed flower. Put sticky-back plastic over the flowers to protect them.

8 Cut two triangles out of bright cardboard or paper. Glue them to the corners of your flower book's front cover for extra decoration.

9 Punch a hole through the cover and the pages on the side where the book opens. Thread ribbon through it and tie in a loose bow.

Slimy, Slithery Pets

Some people do not like slugs and snails. They are put off them because they look slimy and because they cause damage to plants and flowers. But slugs and snails are fascinating creatures. Watch how they extend and contract their legless bodies so that they can glide smoothly over even rough surfaces. See how snails push out the long stalks that their eyes are on. If a snail is threatened it will hide inside its protective shell.

YOU WILL NEED THESE MATERIALS AND TOOLS

No-peat compost (soil mix)

Large plastic drinks bottle

Plate

Twigs

Trowel

Leaves

Scissors

Gardening gloves

Pebbles

Apple

Muslin or cheesecloth

Tile or piece of wood

Rubber band

Lettuce leaves

Tiffani loves watching the snails and slugs in her special minibeast home. Make sure that you put some cloth over the top to stop them crawling out. Smooth, steep sides will not stop agile slugs and snails escaping! The cloth must allow air into the container so that the animals can breathe.

1 Put the lettuce and apple on a plate and place it in the garden among the plants. Cover it with a tile that is resting on four pebbles. Leave overnight.

2 While you wait to see what wanders into your trap, make a minibeast home. Ask an adult to cut a plastic bottle in half.

3 Put compost into the bottom of the bottle. Always wear gardening gloves when working with compost or garden soil.

4 Add lots of leaves and twigs to the container. Juicy leaves will help to keep your minibeast home moist and will give your pets something to eat.

5 Check your trap early in the morning. The slugs and snails might be hiding under the lettuce or even under the plate.

6 Put your new pets carefully into their minibeast home. Try not to squash them as you pick them up. Snails die if their shells are damaged.

What is a mollusc?

The scientific name for slugs, snails and their relatives is molluscs. Squids, octopuses, clams, cockles and mussels are also molluscs. They nearly all have shells. Some molluscs, such as slugs, have small shells inside their bodies. Clams and mussels have two shells that are hinged together like a suitcase.

Slugs and snails move by making the underside of their body ripple. The underside is called the foot. The slime that they leave in their trail is a sort of glue. This helps them to stick to any surface, no matter how smooth or slippery.

Minibeast homes

This is what a good minibeast home should look like. The muslin cover allows air into the container and there is plenty of food for the creatures to eat. Release the animals after one or two days. To keep them any longer would be cruel.

Alf and Freda

Planting seeds and watching them grow is always enjoyable, especially when you can eat what you have grown! Make these two funny characters by planting alfalfa seeds in decorated egg cups. When Alf and Freda's edible hair gets too long, cut it off and add it to salads or sandwiches. When you pour water on to the seeds, watch closely. Can you see the jelly that covers the seeds?

What are seeds?

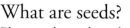

Plants make seeds so that new plants will grow. Inside each seed is a tiny baby plant and enough food for it to start to grow. Seeds are protected by a tough case with a small hole in it. When the seed gets wet, water seeps through this hole so the plant can start to germinate, or grow. A tiny root pushes through the hole and grows down into the soil where it can take in water. Meanwhile, the case splits open and the stem and its leaves grow upwards towards the light. Plants need light to make food so that they can keep growing.

Naeve is not sure which one is Alf and which one is Freda. But she is very pleased with their funny faces and their delicious and nutritious hair!

YOU WILL NEED THESE MATERIALS AND TOOLS

Absorbent kitchen paper

Water

Scissors

Absorbent cotton

Two plain egg cups

Small dot stickers

Sprouting seeds (alfalfa, mung beans, mustard or cress)

Felt-tip pens

Rubber bands

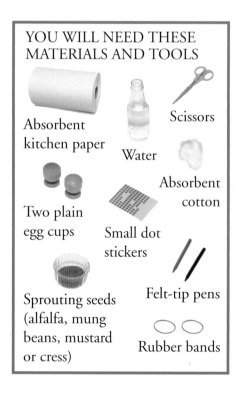

1 Ask an adult for permission to use two egg cups. Stick dots on to the fronts of the egg cups to make the eyes and rosy cheeks.

2 Use the felt-tip pens to draw a nose, mouth, eyebrows, eyelashes and freckles on to the egg cups. Add other details, like glasses, if you want to.

3 Stuff cotton balls into the egg cups. To get the best effect, the absorbent cotton should come almost to the top of the cup.

4 Sprinkle the sprouting seeds on to the cotton balls. To make Alf and Freda's hair really thick, use a lot of seeds and cover the cotton evenly.

5 Moisten the cotton balls very carefully with water. Try not to drown the seeds or wash them away into the bottom of the egg cups.

6 To help the seeds germinate, keep them in the dark for one or two days. Cover them with absorbent paper secured with rubber bands.

7 When the seedlings have come out of the cases, take off the paper and leave the cups on a window sill. Keep the cotton balls damp.

Alf and Freda's curly hair will keep growing if you water them daily and leave them in a light, airy place. The best time to eat the seedlings is when they are young and juicy.

Creative Casts

Create copies of nature's treasures by making moulds and casts. First make a mould of the specimen by pressing it into non-hardening clay. Then fill the mould with plaster-of-Paris. This is a white powder that is mixed with water. It will harden to make a cast of your specimen.

Beachcombing
Beachcombing is great fun. If you are lucky enough to go to the beach, walk along the shore and see what you can find. The bits and pieces that are washed ashore by the waves are called flotsam and jetsam.

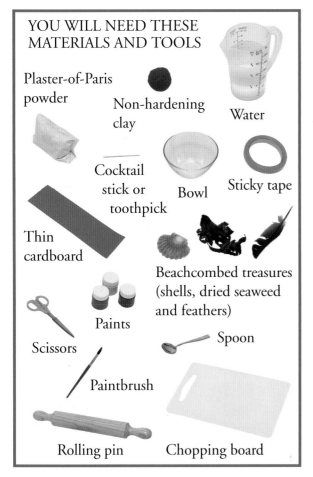

YOU WILL NEED THESE
MATERIALS AND TOOLS

Plaster-of-Paris powder

Non-hardening clay

Water

Cocktail stick or toothpick

Bowl

Sticky tape

Thin cardboard

Beachcombed treasures (shells, dried seaweed and feathers)

Scissors

Paints

Spoon

Paintbrush

Rolling pin

Chopping board

Abayomi holds up his plaster cast of a seashell. He has painted it carefully so that the pretty pattern of the shell's shape really stands out.

1 On the chopping board, roll out the non-hardening clay with the rolling pin. You need to make a smooth thick slab.

2 Press your specimen into the slab quite firmly. Seashells make very good moulds. Try not to move or break your specimen as you press it.

3 Carefully lift your specimen off the slab. It should have left an impression of its shape and pattern in the clay.

4 Bend a strip of cardboard into a ring that will fit around the slab. Secure the ends with tape. Press the bottom edge of the ring into the slab.

5 Make the plaster-of-Paris according to the instructions. So that you do not get lumps, add the water a little at a time and keep stirring.

6 Spoon the mixture into the mould so that it thickly covers the slab. Work quickly so that the plaster does not harden before you have finished.

7 When the plaster has set, undo the sticky tape. Ease the cardboard carefully away from the cast and out of the slab of clay.

8 Lift the plaster cast off the slab of clay. Use a cocktail stick or toothpick to remove any bits of clay that have stuck to the cast.

9 Paint the cast a bright shade. Paint the background of the cast using a different paint so that the specimen really stands out.

Wild Flower Window Box

Make a wild flower meadow on your window ledge. Summer wild flowers are a very important part of the natural world. Many butterflies depend on the leaves of wild flowers as food for their caterpillars. If there are no wild flowers, there will be no butterflies.

Window boxes

This lovely window box is made of a type of clay called terracotta. If you do not have a terracotta pot, use a plastic or wooden one instead. An empty ice-cream container also makes an excellent window box.

You can buy wild flower seeds for your window box from a nursery. Some seeds are specially suited for growing in hedgerows. The best ones for window boxes are meadow flower seeds. When your plants start to grow they may look like weeds. This is because weeds are just very successful wild flowers!

YOU WILL NEED THESE MATERIALS AND TOOLS

Gardening gloves

Trowel

Long window box and no-peat compost (soil mix)

Watering can

Jam jar with lid

Packet of wild flower seeds

Here is Sophie with her finished Wild Flower Window Box. She has kept it well watered and her seeds have grown into flowering plants. Soon they will make their own seeds.

1 Use the trowel to fill the window box carefully with compost. Wear a pair of gardening gloves to keep your hands clean.

2 Water the compost thoroughly before you put the seeds in. The seeds will not germinate, or grow, unless they are wet.

3 Put about one trowel-full of compost into the jam jar. Empty some wild flower seeds into the jar. Replace the lid on the jar.

4 Shake the jam jar to mix the seeds and compost together. This makes it easy to spread the seeds evenly over the surface of the window box.

5 Carefully spread the compost and seed mixture over the wet compost in the window box. The compost in the mixture will cover the seeds.

6 Ask an adult to fix the window box on to a window ledge. You will have to water it everyday, so make sure that you can reach it easily and safely.

7 Watch your plants grow and then bloom into flower. Record in your nature notebook which insects visit your window box.

Helping wild flowers

Many of the places where wild flowers once grew have been turned over to growing crops. Fields and meadows have also been sprayed with weed-killers that causes all the wild flowers to die. Because of these things many wild flowers are becoming very rare.

Help to preserve wild flowers by growing them in a window box or in the garden. Leave the flowers on the plants until they have made their seeds. The seed heads will open and the wind will scatter the seeds.

Bark and Leaf Rubbings

Tree trunks and branches have a thick, protective covering called bark. The bark has patterns of ridges, knobs, slits, twists and holes all over it. The patterns are different on each kind of tree. Leaves also have different shapes and patterns. The easiest way to recognize a tree is by looking at its leaves. Make bark and leaf rubbings to see these shapes and patterns clearly.

Bark

Bark is waterproof and too tough for most animals to eat. It protects the softer wood inside. As trees grow, their trunks and branches get thicker. But the bark on the outside is dead, so it cracks and flakes as new bark grows underneath. It is these cracks that make the different patterns for each tree.

YOU WILL NEED THESE MATERIALS AND TOOLS

Leaves

Drawing pins (thumb tacks)

Thick paper

Wax crayons

Naeve has made a collection of bark and leaf rubbings. She used a different shade of wax crayon for each tree.

1 Find a tree with some knobbly bark. Pin a piece of paper to the tree trunk. Bark is tough, so ask an adult to help you.

2 Use a wax crayon to rub over the paper. Rub just hard enough to allow the pattern to show. Do not press too hard or the paper will tear.

3 Make bark rubbings from different trees. Find some nice fallen leaves from each tree and give them to a friend.

4 Your friend can choose the leaves they like best. Ask your friend to make rubbings of these leaves to go with your bark pictures.

5 To do a leaf rubbing, lay the chosen leaf with its underside face up on a smooth hard surface. Cover it completely with a sheet of paper.

6 Rub a wax crayon over the paper until the leaf vein pattern shows through. Do not press too hard or the pattern will not come out.

7 On the piece of paper, write the name of the leaf and when you did the rubbing. Try more rubbings using leaves from other trees.

8 Notice how the leaves from different trees have a different shape and pattern of veins. The veins will show up clearly on your rubbings.

9 Match the bark rubbings to the leaf rubbings. To keep all the rubbings safe and clean, glue them into a nature notebook.

Tie-dye T-shirt

Tie-dyeing is a way of decorating fabric by tying knots in it to make pretty patterns. The knots prevent the dye from darkening all parts of the fabric. In this project, natural vegetable dyes have been used to decorate the T-shirt. Tie-dying is easy to do and inexpensive.

Natural vegetable dyes

In the past, people always used natural dyes on their fabrics. There were no artificial dyes, as there are today. They used dyes made from plants, fruits and vegetables, and you can too. Choose things like onion skins, red cabbage, blackberries and beetroot. Natural dyes tend to be much paler than modern, artificial ones.

Jack likes the fact that his new tie-dyed T-shirt is unique. Natural vegetable dyes work best on natural fabrics like cotton.

YOU WILL NEED THESE MATERIALS AND TOOLS

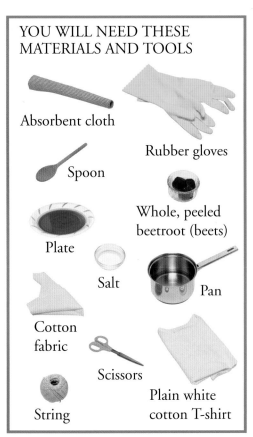

Absorbent cloth

Rubber gloves

Spoon

Whole, peeled beetroot (beets)

Plate

Salt

Pan

Cotton fabric

Scissors

String

Plain white cotton T-shirt

1 Wrap the beetroot in a square of cotton fabric. Beetroot dye can be messy, so make sure that you have a wet cloth nearby to wipe your hands.

2 Tie the fabric with a piece of string so that the beetroot is held in a parcel. Tie the string firmly, but make sure you can undo it later.

3 Put two tablespoons of salt into the pan. Add water and the beetroot parcel. Ask an adult to boil this for 30 minutes. Allow it to cool.

4 Put the T-shirt into the pan and ask an adult to simmer it for 20 minutes. Let the pan and T-shirt cool before taking the T-shirt out.

5 Squeeze out as much liquid as you can into the pan. You must wear rubber gloves or your hands will also turn a pink beetroot shade!

6 Knot the T-shirt, or tie pieces of string tightly around bunches of fabric. Put it back in the dye. Ask an adult to simmer it for 20 minutes.

7 Let the T-shirt dry thoroughly before you undo the knots or untie the strings to see the patterns. Ask an adult to iron it.

This T-shirt was tied up after it had been dyed once, so the lighter areas are pink. You could knot the T-shirt before you put it into the dye and the knotted areas will be white.

Magic Bean Maze

Plants like this bean seedling have no eyes and cannot see. So how do they get through a maze like this one? You might think that it is a magic maze, but you would be wrong. What happens is that plants will always seek the light and grow towards it. They have to do this because, without light, they would die.

Why are plants green?
Plants are green because green is very good for soaking up light. Plants make their own food by using the energy in light. This means that plants must be in the light every day. At night, they can survive on the food that they made during the daytime. This bean seed has enough food stored inside it to last for a few days, until it finds the light.

YOU WILL NEED THESE MATERIALS AND TOOLS

No-peat compost (soil mix)

Water pot

Watering can

Scissors

Shoebox with lid

Gardening gloves

Thin cardboard

Ruler

Trowel

Small plant pot

Black electrical tape

Pencil

Bean seed

Black paint

Paintbrush

This is what your maze should look like before you close the lid and wait for the bean to germinate, or grow.

1 Ask an adult to cut a 2cm/1in hole in the end of the shoebox with a pair of scissors. Stand the box on its end with the hole at the top.

2 Measure and cut a strip of cardboard the same depth as the box and twice as long. Cut the strip into four small and four large rectangles.

3 Tape the strips inside the box to form shelves. The gaps between the shelves must not line up. Leave room for the pot at the bottom of the box.

4 Paint the inside of the box, the shelves and the inside of the lid with black paint. This will make it very dark inside the box.

5 Put some compost into the plant pot with your trowel. Bury the bean seed somewhere in the middle of the compost.

6 Water the plant pot thoroughly. The bean seed must have enough moisture so that it will start growing into a seedling.

Not even a maze could stop this bean from growing towards the light.

7 Put the lid on the box. The only light entering it will come from the hole. Put the box in a warm place and keep the compost watered.

8 The bean will take a few days to grow into a seedling. It will climb through the maze to find the light. The tip will then appear in the hole.

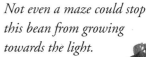

Wiggly Wormery

Worms are easy to look after for a short time. All they need is a container of damp soil in a cool, dark place. Watch how they move about by stretching and squeezing. If you let them crawl over your hand you will feel the rows of bristles that they use to pull themselves through their narrow tunnels.

Nature's gardeners

Earthworms are very important. Their holes and tunnels allow air and water to get down to plant roots. They also mix up all the bits and pieces in the soil to make it fine and loose. Plants grow better in soil like this. You may need an adult to help dig up the worms from the garden. Worms can tunnel very deep and they will move swiftly if they sense they are in danger.

Watch the bands of different soil disappear as the worms tunnel around and mix up the sand and the compost. You may see the sand that they have eaten forming piles on the top of the wormery.

YOU WILL NEED THESE TOOLS AND MATERIALS

Apple

Gardening gloves

No-peat compost (soil mix)

Scissors

Worms

Large plastic drinks bottle

Dead leaves

Trowel

Funnel

Black paper

Sand

Muslin or cheesecloth

Rubber band

Sticky tape

1 Ask an adult to cut around the top of the bottle to make the container. You will need to use a large bottle for this project.

2 Put a layer of compost in the bottom of the container. Then add a layer of sand. Gardening gloves will help to keep your hands clean.

3 Try using a funnel to put the sand into the container. This makes it fall in an even layer, instead of forming a large pile in the middle.

4 Add more layers of compost and sand until just before you reach the top. Put a few dead leaves and a piece of apple on top.

5 Gently transfer your worms to the container. Watch how quickly they dig themselves deep into the layers of compost and sand.

6 Cover the wormery with a square of muslin. Secure the muslin with a large rubber band.

7 Make a cylinder of black paper. Keep it around the wormery when you are not watching the worms. Keep the compost and sand cool and damp.

Worms feed by swallowing soil. They take the food that they need out of the soil. The unwanted soil passes straight through the worm. This helps to mix the soil up. When the soil comes out of the worm, it acts as a rich fertilizer. Fertilizers help plants to grow.

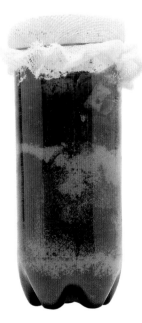

Butterfly Garden

The best way to attract butterflies is to plant a butterfly garden. You could make your garden in a small space, such as the Wild Flower Window Box, or it could be larger, with room for many different plants and herbs. Choose plants that bloom at various times of the year. Different plants attract butterflies and caterpillars, their young. Try not to use insecticides in your part of the garden. When studying butterflies, keep very still. Do not let your shadow fall on the insects or you will frighten them.

YOU WILL NEED THESE MATERIALS AND TOOLS

Gardening gloves

Trowel

Packets of seeds or young plants

Rake

Watering can

Notebook

Pencil

Field guide

Butterfly bush
Buddleia is a very popular plant with butterflies and so it has gained the nickname butterfly bush. It has masses of sweet-smelling mauve or purple flowers. Butterflies that are attracted to buddleia include small tortoiseshells (shown here), peacocks, painted ladies, commas and red admirals.

1 Grow some plants from seed or buy some young plants. Wearing gloves, dig over your chosen patch of soil with a trowel or a spade.

2 Break up any large clods of soil with a rake or spade. Now rake over the top of your plot so that the earth is evenly spread.

3 Dig small holes for your plants with the trowel. Place the plants in the holes and press the soil down firmly with gloved hands.

4 Water the plants well. They will need to be watered regularly throughout the spring and summer. The sun will scorch wet leaves during the day, so water plants at dusk.

5 Record which butterflies you see visiting your flowers. A field guide will help you to identify them. Which species prefer which flowers? Which is the most popular plant?

Caterpillars feed on particular leafy plants, such as grasses, thistles and nettles. Adult moths and butterflies gather on plants with nectar-bearing flowers. Wallflowers, buddleia, goldenrod, candytuft, ice-plants and hebes will attract adult insects. Moths are attracted to honeysuckle because the flowers release a sweet smell at night. You will have to ask a responsible adult if you can grow these plants. Now that you have attracted some butterflies, you can watch their caterpillars transform into beautiful adults in the next project...

Caring for Caterpillars

You can learn a lot about butterfly and moth life cycles by keeping caterpillars. When picking up caterpillars, try not to touch them directly with your fingers, as some species have hairs that may irritate skin. Pick them up with a paintbrush, or encourage them to climb on to a leaf. Carry them home in a collecting jar.

Preferred plants

Look for caterpillars on plants where you see half-eaten leaves and stems. You may find them hiding on the undersides of leaves. Make a careful note of the plant on which you found them and take some leaves with you. The caterpillars of small tortoiseshell butterflies, shown here, feed on stinging nettles. Use your field guide to identify the species you have found. Check the guide to see which plant they prefer. Try to disturb the caterpillars as little as possible while they are in your care.

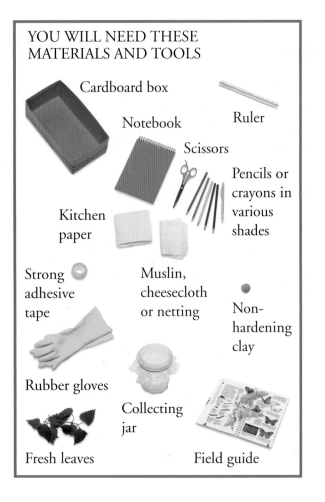

YOU WILL NEED THESE MATERIALS AND TOOLS

Cardboard box

Notebook

Ruler

Scissors

Pencils or crayons in various shades

Kitchen paper

Strong adhesive tape

Muslin, cheesecloth or netting

Non-hardening clay

Rubber gloves

Collecting jar

Fresh leaves

Field guide

When the caterpillars become adult moths or butterflies it is time to let them go. Take the insects back to where you found them. Lift the lid off the box and let them fly away.